To: [redacted]
From: Granny
With love and kisses
xxxx

This book belongs to:

Reuben +

Isaac

A Treasury for Four Year Olds

A Treasury for Four Year Olds

A Collection of Stories, Fairytales and Nursery Rhymes

p

Language Consultant: Betty Root.

This is a Parragon book
This edition published in 2006

Parragon
Queen Street House
4 Queen Street
Bath BA1 1HE, UK

Copyright © Parragon Books Ltd 2001

All rights reserved. No part of this publication may be reproduced, stored in a retrieval system, or transmitted by any means, electronic, mechanical, photocopying, recording, or otherwise, without the prior permission of the copyright holder.

Printed in China

1-40546-890-4

✦ Contents ✦

The Fast and Flashy Fish
by Nicola Baxter
12

Henny-Penny
retold by Gabriella Goldsack
19

Here We Go Round the
Mulberry Bush
24

The Wolf and the Raccoon
by Alison Boyle
26

The Naughty Little Rabbits
by Judy Hindley
32

Little Bo-Peep
and other farmyard rhymes
38

Tom Thumb
by the Brothers Grimm
retold by Gabriella Goldsack
40

Ug-Ug-Ugly
by Alison Boyle
48

Old Mother Hubbard
55

The Three Billy Goats Gruff
retold by Gabriella Goldsack
58

The Frog Prince
by the Brothers Grimm
retold by Gabriella Goldsack
64

Runaway Ragtime
by David R. Morgan
71

One, Two, Buckle My Shoe
78

The Three Little Pigs
and the Wolf
by Alison Boyle
80

Polly Penguin Wants to Fly
by Gill Davies
86

Wee Willie Winkie
and other goodnight rhymes
92

The Fast and Flashy Fish

Swish!

What was that? The warm, blue waters of the Indian Ocean are full of colourful creatures. There are tiny little yellow fish. There are long thin purple fish.

There are wiggly worms who pretend to be flowers – and flowers who pretend to be wiggly worms. Everything waves and sways in the sea. But,

swish! Somebody is never still. A fast and flashy fish whizzes through the water all day long. He moves so quickly that you can hardly see him. But you can hear him!

Swish! Wish!

"I'm the fastest fish!
No one catches me
In the deep, blue sea!"
That is what the fast and flashy fish sings over and over again.

He wiggles his fins at a starfish. "Let's race, jelly face!" he cries.

"Ready, steady, swim!"

"But!" says the starfish. The fast and flashy fish doesn't hear her.

Swish! He is already five rocks away and laughing.

Swish! Wish!

"I'm the fastest fish!
No one catches me
In the deep, blue sea!"

Still, it's not much fun racing an anemone who hardly moves. Under the rocks, the fish sees someone scuttling along.

"Aha!" says the fast and flashy fish. "It's a lobster! Let's have a race, crabby claws! Ready, steady, swim!"

"Hey!" says the lobster, lumbering onto the rock. The fast and flashy fish doesn't hear him.

Swish!

He has already reached the other side of an old wreck and is giggling to himself.

Swish! Wish!

"I'm the fastest fish!
No one catches me
In the deep, blue sea!"

The lobster is still complaining but he's too far away to hear. The fast and flashy fish looks around for someone else to have fun with.

From out of the wreck comes one waving, wiggling leg. Then there are two waving, wiggling legs. Then, three, four, five, six, seven . . . eight waving, wiggling legs! It's a large pink and orange octopus!

"Ho! Ho!" says the fast and flashy fish. "This is more like it! Let's have a race, loopy legs! Ready, steady, swim!"

"I'm not," says the octopus crossly, but

swish!

The fast and flashy fish is already out in the middle of the coral reef, safe among its beautiful branches.

Swish! Wish!

"I'm the fastest fish!
No one catches me
In the deep, blue sea!"

"It's a pity I can't find someone better to race," grumbles the fast and flashy fish. "This is so boring."

"How about me?" booms a deep, bubbling voice. Overhead, a huge, fat fish is floating. "Come out of the coral," he says, "and we'll see who's the fastest fish."

So the fast and flashy fish

swims up to the big fish. "No problem, flabby fins," he says. "Are you . . . ready, steady!"

"Wait!" glugs the big fish. "This isn't fair. We must line up, nose to nose. Come along."

But when the fast and flashy fish lines up beside the fat and floating fish, the bigger fish complains.

"I can't see what you're doing there. I'm quite happy for you to have a bit of a start. Line your tail up in front of my nose and then I can see where you are."

The fast and flashy fish laughs and swishes. "No problem, froggy face!" he cries.

"Ready, steady!"

"No," says the big fish. "I'll say it. Ready, steady . . . gulp!"

The fast and flashy fish has not been seen for a long time in the warm, blue waters of the Indian Ocean. But sometimes, when a huge, fat fish comes floating by, a tiny voice can be heard.

Swish! Wish!

"I'm the fastest fish! In the deep, blue sea!"

How dark it can be, Gulp!

Henny-Penny

It was a quiet day in the country. In the farmyard, Henny-Penny was busy pecking around for corn. "It's very boring here," clucked Henny-Penny. "Nothing exciting ever happens." But just then, PLONK, an acorn fell on her head.

"Goodness gracious!" clucked Henny-Penny. "The sky is falling in. I must go and tell the king at once." So away she rushed to tell the king. Before she had gone very far, she bumped into her friend Cocky-Locky.

"Where are you going in such a hurry?" clucked Cocky-Locky.

"The sky is falling in," explained Henny-Penny, "and I'm off to tell the king."

"Well, I'm coming with you," said Cocky-Locky, trotting along behind Henny-Penny. Before they had gone much farther, they bumped into their friend Ducky-Lucky.

"Where are you going in such a hurry?" quacked Ducky-Lucky.

"The sky is falling in," explained Henny-Penny, "and we're off to tell the king."

"Well, I'm coming with you," said Ducky-Lucky, waddling along behind Henny-Penny and Cocky-Locky. They hadn't gone far, when they met their friend Goosey-Loosey.

"Where are you going in such a hurry?" gobbled Goosey-Loosey.

"The sky is falling in," explained Henny-Penny, "and we're off to tell the king."

"Well, I'm coming with you," said Goosey-Loosey, swaying along behind Henny-Penny, Cocky-Locky and Ducky-Lucky. What a strange sight they made!

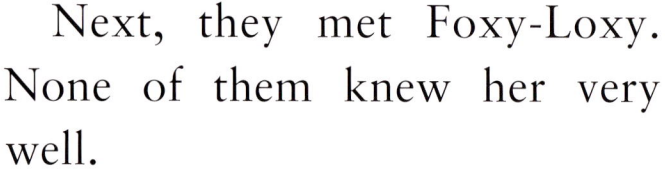

Next, they met Foxy-Loxy. None of them knew her very well.

"Where are you going in such a hurry?" asked Foxy-Loxy.

"The sky is falling in," explained Henny-Penny, "and we're off to tell the king."

"Ah," smiled Foxy-Loxy. "You're going the wrong way. Follow me, I'll show you the way."

"What a nice fox!" clucked Henny-Penny, as she and her three friends followed Foxy-Loxy. On and on they followed her until they reached a cave.

"This is a short cut," said Foxy-Loxy. "Don't be afraid and stay close to me."

The unlucky birds didn't know it, but this wasn't really a short cut – it was Foxy-Loxy's den.

Next, Goosey-Loosey, Ducky-Lucky and Cocky-Locky quickly followed Foxy-Loxy into the cave.

Henny-Penny was about to join them when,

cOcK-A-DOODLE-DOO!

Cocky-Locky let out a terrible scream.

Henny-Penny ran as fast as she could until she reached the safety of the farmyard. Meanwhile, Foxy-Loxy made a fine feast out of Cocky-Locky, Ducky-Lucky and Goosey-Loosey.

Henny-Penny never did get to tell the king that the sky was falling in. But, then again, the sky never was falling in, was it? Wasn't Henny-Penny a silly hen?

Here We Go Round the Mulberry Bush

Here we go round the mulberry bush,
The mulberry bush, the mulberry bush,
Here we go round the mulberry bush,
On a cold and frosty morning.

This is the way we wash our hands,
Wash our hands, wash our hands,
This is the way we wash our hands,
On a cold and frosty morning.

This is the way we brush our hair,
Brush our hair, brush our hair,
This is the way we brush our hair,
On a cold and frosty morning.

This is the way we go to school,
Go to school, go to school,
This is the way we go to school,
On a cold and frosty morning.

The Wolf and the Raccoon

The wind howled and the wind moaned. The wolf tucked her big brush tail around her face even more tightly, sheltering her delicate eyes and delicate nose-tip from the cruel winter. Inside her thick fur were tiny, warm pockets of air that protected her from the cold, just like a duvet.

Wolf slept and, as she slept, the snow fell heavy from the dull white snowclouds and landed along the green branches that criss-crossed above.

A small furry ball of a creature came scampering across the hard woody branches, skimming the prickly needles. Along she came, hopping and skipping, tripping lightly on delicate feet. She was a raccoon,

ears pert, looking for entertainment.

Raccoon spotted Wolf and stopped. She tipped her head this way and that, wondering about a trick, and before she knew it she had turned a quick somersault, landed back on the snow-laden branch – and catapulted a big clump of snow onto the wolf's head.

BOING! THWACK!

"Eer! Eer!"

Wolf jumped up with a start. She cowered low, darting her eyes this way and that to find her attacker. But she could see nothing, and retreated to the shelter of a thick tree-trunk, her eyes sharp, looking every way – except up.

THWACK!

Another clump of snow landed squarely on her head. This time she looked up. There was the cheeky-faced raccoon with her ringed tail, dark-furred eyes and soft black nose.

"Grrrah!" roared the wolf.

"Grrrah!" mimicked the raccoon, feeling safe up the tree.

But wolves can climb too if they have to, and this wolf had to! She aimed for the lowest branch with her thick-

clawed paws, and dragged herself up to a place just underneath Raccoon.

But the raccoon was still smiling. And before jumping higher onto the next branch, she brushed her ringed tail delicately over a snow-clump, sending a shower of speckles down onto the wolf's face.

"Shrrrrrrrr!" screeched Wolf, who was so angry that she leapt even higher up the tree.

And so the two furry creatures jumped up and across and down and along, moving through the great fir trees with such pace that all the other creatures of the forest had a thoroughly bad time of it.

"Oouch!" complained the snowy owls, as they were flicked in their beaks by a twanging branch.

"Brrrrrr!" complained the deer, huddled up close, trying to get comfortable against the cold.

"Cooeeeee!" called the playful beavers, who wanted

to join in. But their father held them back, saying that this was a grown-up game.

"SHFFFFRRRRR!" roared Wolf ferociously.

"Eer! Eer!" mocked Raccoon from high in a tree.

But soon the two creatures stood panting. Raccoon was clamped safely onto a branch with her tail twisted round it, and Wolf was dangerously perched on a branch too thin for her weight. The branch was bending more and more by the moment, until,

"SPROING!"

– it sprang back and catapulted Wolf in a high arc through the air, up to the place where Raccoon was gathering her breath.

"EEEeeeeK!" both creatures cried together as

they collided and fell headlong down the height of the giant fir tree and far to the ground.

But they didn't hurt themselves. Instead, the wolf and the raccoon landed in a heap on a white padded duvet of snow. They looked at one another in silence, while all around the wind moaned and the wind howled. The swirling cold of the wintry forest crept slowly, slowly through the warm pockets of fur on their backs, even reaching their skin.

Their eyes stung. Their noses turned blue. And Wolf and Raccoon started to giggle.

"Shall we save our energy?" suggested the wolf.

"Oh yes indeed," said the raccoon.

The two furry creatures intertwined tails in an instant, tucked their delicate eyes and pointed noses deep down into their shared fur, and slept through another night of winter, until morning, when at last spring began.

The Naughty Little Rabbits

Three little rabbits lived with their mama in a cosy burrow on a hillside. When they were hungry, Mama took them upstairs to nibble on the meadow grass. She showed them games, like Bunny Hop and Rolling-Down-the-Hill. At night, she tucked them up safe in their sleeping corners, down in the deep, dim burrow.

Each little rabbit had its own cosy sleeping corner, which had been dug out of the side of the burrow. It was very snug. The rabbits liked to nestle in their corners, and listen to their mama while she worked at night. She would sweep out the burrow and make everything tidy, murmuring a soft little rabbit lullaby.

But one day, Mama said, "Oh, my! You're getting bigger and taller every day! Soon, you won't fit into your corners. We need to scrape and scrabble, and make them bigger. Come and help me, you three!"

"No, no, no!" cried the little rabbits. "Come upstairs in the sunshine and play with us!"

"First, there is work to do," their mama said. "If you help me, I can come with you. I will show you lots of lovely games. I will find delicious things for us to eat. But first I need you to help me do this work!"

But the naughty little rabbits wouldn't listen. "No! No! No!" they cried. And off they ran, upstairs and out of the burrow.

They had never been outside before without their mama. Now, here they were, out in the big bright meadow, with nothing to do and nobody to play with.

"I don't know what to

do," said the first little rabbit. "I wish we had someone to play with."

Just then, a squirrel ran out of the wood at the edge of the meadow.

"Come and play with me," cried the squirrel. "I know lots of games. Just come along with me, and do what I do."

So they did.

The squirrel ran, and jumped right over a stone. So did the little rabbits.

The squirrel ran, and jumped off the end of a log. So did the little rabbits.

The squirrel ran, and zipped right up a tree.

"Oh, no!" cried the little rabbits.

The Naughty Little Rabbits

"Yah, yah! Got you!" cried the squirrel. It laughed and jeered at the little rabbits down below. Then, it began to throw hard little acorns on top of their heads.

"Ow, ow, ow!" cried the little rabbits. They all ran away, as fast they could go.

When the little rabbits stopped, they were at the bottom of the hill, next to a river.

"Oh, I'm hungry," said the second little rabbit. "I wish we had something to eat."

Just then, a frog popped out of the river. "Come and have lunch with me," said the frog. "I have lots of things to eat. Just do what I do."

The little rabbits gathered round.

"Sit very still," said the frog. So they did.

"Close your eyes," said the frog. So they did.

"Put out your tongues," said the frog.

"YUM!" said the frog, as he swallowed a big, fat fly.

"Yuck! Yuck! Yuck!" cried the little rabbits.

They coughed and spat until they were all worn out.

"I'm so tired," said the third little rabbit. "I wish we could have a cosy nap."

A cloud came over the sun, and it grew dark. It became cold. Rain started to fall.

Plop! Plop! Plop! came the raindrops.

"Help! Oh help!" cried the little rabbits.

Just then, they heard a tiny voice from near their toes. It was a snail.

"You should do what I do," said the snail. "I'm going straight inside."

"Can we come with you?" asked the little rabbits.

The Naughty Little Rabbits

"No," said the snail. "There is only room for me." He popped inside his shell, and was gone.

Then the little rabbits all ran home. They ran and ran, through the dark and the rain, until they were all back safe inside their burrow.

And there was their kind, soft mama waiting for them.

"Sorry, sorry, sorry!" cried the three little rabbits. "Please, can we help you with the work?"

But their mama said, "My dears, you are growing and growing. There will be plenty of work for you to do. But now you must wash your ears and nibble up your supper."

The hungry, sleepy little rabbits washed their ears. They nibbled up their supper. Then they each crawled into their sleeping corners.

And guess what? Someone had made each one just a little bit bigger.

Now who do you think had done that?

Little Bo-Peep

Little Bo-Peep has lost her sheep
And doesn't know where to find them.
Leave them alone and they'll come home
Bringing their tails behind them.

Three Blind Mice

Three blind mice, three blind mice!
See how they run, see how they run!
They all ran after the farmer's wife,
Who cut off their tails with a carving knife,
Did you ever hear such a thing in your life,
As three blind mice?

Mary Had a Little Lamb

Mary had a little lamb,
Its fleece was white as snow,
And everywhere that Mary went
The lamb was sure to go.
It followed her to school one day,
That was against the rule;
It made the children laugh and play
To see a lamb in school.

Tom Thumb

Late one night, a poor farmer and his wife sat talking in their kitchen. "It is a shame we have no children," said the farmer.

"Oh yes, dear," agreed his wife. "I'd be happy if we had just one child. I'd love that child even if it was no bigger than my thumb."

Not long after that, the wife's wish was granted. She gave birth to a baby boy. He was strong and healthy, but he was no bigger than her thumb. The couple were delighted and called their new baby Tom Thumb.

The years passed, but tiny Tom stayed the same size as the day he was born. Although he was very small, Tom was clever and helpful.

One day, the farmer was getting ready to go into the forest to cut wood. "If only I had someone to bring the cart along later," he sighed.

"I'll bring it," said Tom Thumb.

"But Tom," laughed his father. "You're far too small!"

"Don't worry," said Tom Thumb. "Just get Mother to harness the horse and I'll do the rest."

Later, after his mother had harnessed the horse, Tom asked her to place him inside the horse's ear. From there, Tom told the horse where to go. All went well, and soon Tom and the cart had reached the wood. Then, as Tom was shouting "Steady! Steady!", two strangers walked past.

"That's funny!" said one. "I can hear someone directing that cart. Yet nobody is there. Let's see where it goes."

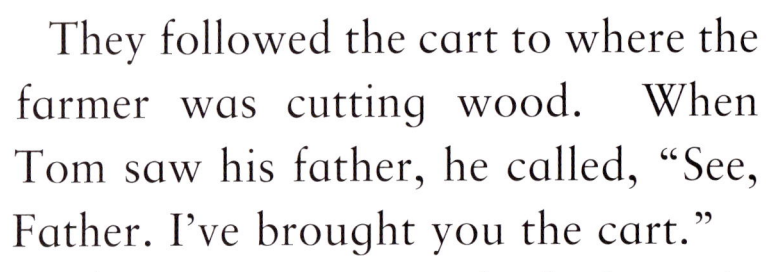

They followed the cart to where the farmer was cutting wood. When Tom saw his father, he called, "See, Father. I've brought you the cart."

The two strangers looked on in astonishment as Tom's father pulled Tom out of the horse's ear. "That little chap could make us our fortune," whispered one of the strangers. "We could take him from town to town and people would pay us to see him."

So the two strangers went up to the farmer and asked, "How much do you want for the little man?"

"I wouldn't sell him for all the gold in the world," replied the farmer.

However, on hearing the strangers' words, Tom had an idea. He climbed onto his father's shoulder and whispered into his ear, "Take their money. I'll soon come back." So the farmer gave Tom to the two strangers, and received a large bag of gold coins in return.

After saying goodbye to his father, Tom was carried off by

the strangers.

They walked for a while until Tom said, "Put me down!" When the man did as Tom asked, the tiny boy ran off and hid in a mouse-hole.

"Goodbye!" shouted Tom. "You should have kept a closer eye on me."

The two men searched for Tom but it was no good. At last, they gave up and went home without him. Tom crept out of the mouse-hole and walked along the path until he found a barn, where he went to sleep in the hay.

The next morning, the milkmaid got up to feed the cows. She went to the barn and grabbed an armful of hay – the same hay in which Tom was sleeping. Poor Tom knew nothing about it, until he found himself inside the stomach of one of the cows.

It was a dark place. And more and more hay kept coming into the cow's stomach. The space left for Tom grew smaller and smaller. At last, Tom cried, "No more hay!"

The milkmaid ran to the dairy farmer in fright. "Sir, the cow is talking," she cried.

"Are you mad?" asked the farmer, but he went to the barn to see for himself.

"No more hay!" shouted Tom. This bewildered the farmer, who sent for the vet.

The vet operated on the cow and out popped a bunch of hay. Tom was hidden inside it. The hay was thrown onto the manure heap. Just as Tom was preparing to escape, a hungry wolf ran by and gulped down Tom and the hay.

Refusing to give up hope, Tom spoke to the wolf, "I know where you can get a mighty feast."

"Where?" asked the wolf.

Quickly, Tom described the way to his father's house.

That night, the wolf climbed in through the farmer's

◆ *A Treasury for Four Year Olds*

kitchen window. Once inside, he ate so much food and grew so fat that he couldn't squeeze back out of the window. This was just what Tom had planned. He began to jump around in the wolf's stomach and shout as loud as he could.

Very soon, the farmer and his wife were awoken by the noise. They rushed into the kitchen. Seeing the wolf, the farmer grabbed his axe and aimed at the wolf. Suddenly he heard Tom's voice, "Father, I am inside the wolf's stomach."

Overjoyed, the farmer killed the wolf with a single blow to his head. Then he cut Tom out of its stomach.

From that day onwards, Tom stayed at home with his parents. Now he knew for sure that there is no place like home!

Ug-Ug-Ugly

Long, long, long ago, a huge egg lay in a nest. The egg wobbled, then wobbled a bit more. It rolled a bit, then rolled a bit more. It rolled right over the edge of the nest – wooooooooo!

Bump! Crack! Plick! Out popped a wrinkly, bobble-eyed, ugly-faced baby dinosaur. He squinted at the wide world all around. Everything looked scary. Through the leaves peeped one, two, three, four wrinkly, bobble-eyed, ugly-faced toddler dinosaurs. They stared at the new baby as he began to wriggle out of his eggshell.

"Ug!" said the first toddler.

"Ug!" said the second.

"Ug!" said the third.

"Ug!" said the fourth, nodding her head. "You're UGLY!"

The baby dinosaur stood up on his thin new legs, and crept away into the shadow of a dark drooping flower.

The toddler dinosaurs skipped off happily, calling:

"Bye for now!"

"Little monster!"

"Come and find us!"

"See you soon!"

Then through the trees burst a wrinkly, bobble-eyed, ugly-faced mummy dinosaur.

"La-di-da!" sang Mummy, "my egg should be hatched by now – la-di-da!"

But when she peered into her nest,

"Uh?" said Mummy. "Where's my baby?"

And **thump! thump! thump!** she trudged off through the steamy forest to look for him. She thumped round the bursting volcano, across the gushing river and through the gurgling swamp, but she couldn't find her baby anywhere.

So Mummy sat down and frowned, and forced her pea-sized brain to think. And think it did. It thought about an egg. It thought about an eggshell.

"EGGSHELL!" she exclaimed, as she thump, thump, thumped back through the gurgling swamp, across the gushing river, round the bursting volcano and through the steamy forest to the place where she had built her nest.

This time she didn't look inside the nest, but on the

ground below it.

"Eggshell!" she whispered, when she spotted a fleck of shiny green shell.

"Eggshell!" she announced, when she spotted more flecks of shell farther along.

"Uh?" said Mummy when the trail of eggshell stopped.

She sat down and frowned, and forced her pea-sized brain to think. And think it did. It thought about a baby.

"WHERE'S MY BABY?" called Mummy at the top of her voice.

"Here we are!" replied her four wrinkly, bobble-eyed, ugly-faced toddler dinosaurs.

"You're not babies!" she said. "I'm talking about the baby who came out of that eggshell. He must be here somewhere."

The toddlers all

silently pointed towards the same place.

Mummy dinosaur gently lifted the head of a dark drooping flower and, curled up in a ball, was her baby.

"Ug!" said the first toddler.

"Ug!" began the second, before Mummy interrupted.

"My baby!" Mummy cried, as she gathered the dinosaur in her huge claws. She looked round proudly at all her ugly children. "Isn't he lovely?" admired Mummy. "What shall we call him?"

"Ugly?" suggested one of the toddlers.

"Don't be so unkind!" scolded Mummy, stroking her newly hatched baby. "Poor little thing – fancy thinking of that!"

"Eggshell?" suggested another, as the baby gurgled loudly.

"He likes that name!" all the toddler dinosaurs called out together.

Mummy sat down and frowned, and forced her pea-sized brain to think. And think it did. It thought about a perfect name for her baby dinosaur. It thought of the long journey Mummy had made to find him.

And the name she came up with was . . .

"GURGLING SWAMP!"

She called out the name at the top of her voice, as the baby gave a huge burp.

"Yeah!" cheered the toddlers, who thought this was a very good name for the wrinkly, bobble-eyed, ugly-faced baby dinosaur who was happily burping (or gurgling) in his mummy's arms.

Old Mother Hubbard

Old Mother Hubbard,
She went to the cupboard
To fetch her poor dog a bone;
But when she got there,
The cupboard was bare,
And so the poor dog had none.

She went to the baker's
To buy him some bread;
But when she came back
The poor dog was dead.

She went to the joiner's
To buy him a coffin;
But when she came back
The poor dog was laughing.

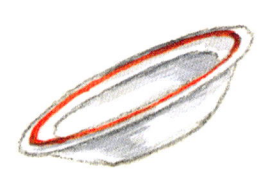

She took a clean dish
To get him some tripe;
But when she came back
He was smoking a pipe.

She went to the fruiterer's
To buy him some fruit;
But when she came back
He was playing the flute.

She went to the tailor's
To buy him a coat;
But when she came back
He was riding a goat.

She went to the cobbler's
To buy him some shoes;
But when she came back
He was reading the news.

She went to the barber's
To buy him a wig;
But when she came back
He was dancing a jig.

She went to the hosier's
To buy him some hose;
But when she came back
He was dressed in his clothes.

She went to the hatter's
To buy him a hat;
But when she came back
He was feeding the cat.

The dame made a curtsey,
The dog made a bow;
The dame said, "Your servant",
The dog said, "Bow-wow".

The Three Billy Goats Gruff

Once, high in some faraway mountains, lived three Billy Goats Gruff. There was a teeny, tiny billy goat, a middle-sized billy goat and a big, strong billy goat.

One day, when the teeny, tiny Billy Goat Gruff was searching for some juicy grass to eat, he noticed a meadow full of green, green grass on the other side of the river. "Hmm," he thought, "if I could just cross over that bridge and eat some of that grass I could grow as big as my brothers."

But every smart Billy Goat Gruff knew that an ugly troll lived under the bridge. A troll who was so bad and ugly that any goat who dared to set foot on the bridge was never heard of again.

"I've never seen him," thought the teeny, tiny Billy Goat Gruff. "Perhaps he's moved away. That grass looks so very delicious, I think I'll just tiptoe across and hope for the best!"

So the brave little Billy Goat Gruff tiptoed his way across the bridge.

TRIP, TRAP! TRIP, TRAP! TRIP, TRAP!

went his hooves. He was halfway across the bridge when suddenly, "ROAR", out jumped the horrible troll. "Who's that trip, trapping over my bridge?" roared the troll.

"Only little old me," said the teeny, tiny Billy Goat Gruff. "I'm on my way to the meadow to eat grass. Don't let me disturb you."

"Oh, no, you don't," roared the ugly troll. "You've woken me up and now I'm going to gobble you up."

"But I'm just a skinny thing," said the teeny, tiny Billy Goat Gruff. "Hardly a snack really. Why don't you wait for my middle-sized brother to come along? There's far more meat on him."

"Okay, okay," roared the nasty troll. "Now hurry along before I change my mind."

Later, when the middle-sized Billy Goat Gruff saw his teeny, tiny brother enjoying the green, green grass on the other side of the bridge, he decided to join him.

TRIP, TRAP!
TRIP, TRAP!
TRIP, TRAP!

went his hooves as he tiptoed over the bridge.

But he was only halfway across, when, "ROAR", out jumped the evil troll. "Who's that trip, trapping over my bridge?" he roared.

"Only me," said the middle-sized Billy Goat Gruff. "I'm off to the far meadow to eat green grass. I hope I didn't wake you."

"Oh, no, you don't," roared the nasty troll. "You've disturbed me while I'm fishing, and now I'm going to gobble you up."

"But I'm not very big," said the middle-sized Billy Goat Gruff. "I'm all coat really. Why don't you wait for my big brother to come along? He's big and fat. He would make you a proper feast."

"Alright," roared the troll. "But hurry up before I change my mind."

The big Billy Goat Gruff could hardly believe his

eyes when he saw his brothers enjoying the green, green grass on the other side of the bridge. "They will finish it all if I'm not quick," he thought, as he tiptoed his way across the bridge. But he had barely gone more than a few paces before,

"ROAR", out leapt the horrible troll.

"Who's that trip, trapping over my bridge?" roared the troll.

"Just me," said the big Billy Goat Gruff. "I'm on my way to the meadow to eat grass."

"Oh, no, you're not!" roared the troll. "I've heard all about you and now I'm going to gobble you up."

"Oh, no, you're not," roared the biggest Billy Goat Gruff. Then he lowered his horns and charged!

"Ahhhh!" screamed the nasty troll, as the biggest Billy Goat Gruff tossed him into the air. "Heeelp!" he screamed, as he flew higher and higher, until, SPLASH, he fell into the deepest part of the river.

Without looking back, the biggest Billy Goat Gruff raced to join his brothers. And from that day onwards the three Billy Goats Gruff and all their friends could cross over the bridge to eat the green, green grass whenever they wanted. As for the troll, well no one ever heard of him again.

The Frog Prince

Once upon a time, there lived a young princess. She had lots and lots of toys but her favourite one was a golden ball. She carried it with her wherever she went.

One day the princess set off for a walk in the woods. When she grew tired, she sat down beside a pool to rest. As she sat there, she threw her golden ball into the air and caught it. Higher and higher she threw the ball, until one time it soared so high that she couldn't catch it. SPLASH! The ball fell into the pool. The princess peered into the dark water but it was so deep that she couldn't see the bottom.

"Oh, no!" wailed the princess. "My ball is lost. I

would give anything – even my fine clothes and jewels – just anything to have my ball back."

Just then she heard a noise,

"RIBBET! RIBBET!"

A frog popped its ugly head out of the water and spoke, "Dear Princess, what is wrong? Why are you crying?"

"Eeeek!" screamed the princess. She was not used to meeting frogs that could talk. "Wh . . . what can a nasty frog do to help me? My golden ball has fallen into the pool. Now it is gone for ever!"

"Don't cry," croaked the frog. "If you will just let me eat from your plate and sleep on your pillow, I will find your ball."

"Hmm!" thought the princess. "This slimy frog will never be able to get out of the water. If it finds my ball, I won't have to do any of those silly things." So she turned to the frog and lied, "If you bring back my ball, I promise to do everything you ask."

At that, the frog ducked beneath the water. In no time at all, he was back with the ball in his mouth. He threw it at the princess's feet. Delighted, the princess snatched up the ball and ran home as fast as she could. Not once did she think to say thank-you to the frog. Indeed, she forgot all about him.

"Wait for me!" croaked the frog. But the princess was gone.

The next evening, as the princess sat down to dinner, she heard a strange noise:

PLISH, PLASH, PLISH!

It sounded as if something wet was coming up the stairs. Then there was a TAP, TAP on the door and a little voice croaked,

"Open the door, my one true love.
Open the door, my turtle dove.
Remember the promise you made in the wood
Well now is the time to make it come good."

The princess opened the door and there stood the frog. Feeling frightened, she slammed the door in his face.

"What's the matter?" asked her father, the king.

The princess told him all about her lost ball and her promise to the frog.

"You must always keep a promise, my dear," the king said to his daughter.

"Go and let him in." So the princess opened the door.

The frog hopped in and —PLISH, PLASH, PLISH!— made his way to the table.

"Lift me up to sit beside you," said the frog. Wrinkling her nose, the princess did as he asked.

"Push your plate closer so that I can eat from it," said the frog. Closing her eyes, the princess did as he asked. When the frog had eaten as much as he could, he croaked, "I'm tired. Carry me upstairs and let me sleep in your bed." With a large frown on her face, the princess did as he asked.

Within minutes, the frog was snoring away on the princess's pillow.

And there he slept until it was morning. Then he

zzZZZ zZZZ

awoke and hopped away without so much as a RIBBET. "Hooray!" cried the princess. "That should be the last I see of that jumped-up tadpole."

But the princess was wrong. That evening, the frog knocked on the door once more, and croaked,

"Open the door, my one true love.
Open the door, my turtle dove.
Remember the promise you made in the wood.
Well now is the time to make it come good."

The princess opened the door and –

PLISH, PLASH, PLISH!

– in hopped the frog.

Once again, he ate from the princess's plate and slept on her pillow until morning.

By the third evening, the princess was beginning to like the frog a little. "His eyes are quite lovely," she thought, as she drifted off to sleep.

But when the princess awoke the next morning, she was astonished to find a handsome prince standing beside her bed. The frog was nowhere to be seen. As she gazed into the prince's strangely familiar eyes, he explained how an evil fairy had cast a spell on him and turned him into an ugly frog. The spell could only be broken when a princess let him eat from her plate and sleep in her bed for three nights.

"Now you have broken the spell, and I wish to ask for your hand in marriage," said the prince.

Being a princess, she quickly agreed, and before the prince could say "RIBBET", a fine coach and a handsome horse appeared. Together they rode off to the prince's home where they lived happily ever after.

Runaway Ragtime

Ragtime was a large black-and-white cat who lived in a busy town. He loved his town, with its winding side streets, its busy supermarkets and its delicious dustbins.

So when Ragtime's family, the Pips, moved to the country, Ragtime wasn't at all happy. He didn't like it one little bit. He didn't like the trees. He didn't like the fields. He didn't like the streams.

One morning, Ragtime was feeling really bored. Mrs Pip had gone off to work and Mr Pip was taking Thomas and Tillie to school. Ragtime decided to climb over the garden fence into the field behind. He was running away to have an adventure.

Ragtime hadn't got far when he bumped into a blackbird, which was juggling pebbles on its beak. "Hello!" said Ragtime. "I'm Runaway Ragtime. I'm having an adventure."

"Hello!" squawked the blackbird. "I'm Beaker. Can I come too?"

"Of course!" replied Ragtime, and the two new friends set off together. Soon Ragtime and Beaker reached a babbling stream. Suddenly a frog appeared out of the reeds, doing cartwheels.

"Hello!" said Ragtime. "I'm Runaway Ragtime. I'm having an adventure."

"And I'm Beaker," squawked Beaker. "I juggle pebbles on my beak."

"Hello!" gulped the frog. "I'm Monica. I can do cartwheels. Can I come too?"

"Of course!" replied Ragtime, and the three friends set off together.

As they crossed a plank over the stream, they discovered a duck whistling a tune.

"Hello!" said Ragtime. "I'm Runaway Ragtime. I'm having an adventure."

"Hello!" squawked the blackbird. "I'm Beaker. I juggle pebbles on my beak."

"Hello!" said Monica. "I'm Monica, the cartwheeling frog."

"Well done!" quacked the duck. "I'm Ronda. I whistle tunes. Can I come too?"

And so the four friends set off together towards the wood, where they chanced upon a dancing mouse and a smiling snail.

"Hello!" said Ragtime. "I'm Runaway Ragtime. I'm having an adventure."

"Yes!" squawked Beaker. "I'm Beaker, and I juggle pebbles on my beak."

"Hello!" said Monica. "I'm Monica, and I do cartwheels."

"That's true," quacked Ronda. "I'm Ronda. Listen to me whistle."

"That's good," squeaked the mouse.

"I'm Didgeri, and this is Angelo. He's a very talented snail. We like adventures. Can we come too?"

"Of course!" replied Ragtime, and all the friends set off together. They made their way through some tall trees and came to a farm. In the meadow beside the farmhouse stood a very large bull.

"Hello!" said Ragtime. "I'm Runaway Ragtime, and these are my new friends. We're all having an adventure."

"Yes!" squawked Beaker. "I'm Beaker. I juggle pebbles on my beak."

"Hello!" said Monica. "I'm Monica. I do cartwheels."

"That's true," quacked Ronda. "I'm Ronda. I whistle tunes."

"Hello!" squeaked Didgeri. "I'm Didgeri, I dance. And this is Angelo, a very talented snail."

"Oh, that's nice. Lovely. So you're all having an adventure," snorted the bull. "I'm Barney McCabe."

Barney's horns glistened in the afternoon sun.

"Now run for your lives!"

Runaway Ragtime swung around as Beaker flew up into the air showering pebbles everywhere. One of the pebbles whizzed past Monica as she was cartwheeling away. On and on it whizzed, past whistling Ronda and squeaking Didgeri with the very talented Angelo sliding along as fast as he could.

What a chase it was! Snort! Meow! Squawk! Gulp! Quack! Whistle! Squeak! Hah! Pah!

Boing! Snort! WHAT A CHASE!

And all the time Barney McCabe was catching up, catching up . . . CATCHING UP the talented band as across the meadow, through the wood, over the stream and into the field they ran. HELP!

As they raced into the field Ragtime recognized something familiar – HOME! The home that was so boring he'd run away from it, but oh how pleased he was to see it now!

First Ragtime, and then all his friends, dashed, flew, cartwheeled, bounced, danced and hopped over the fence. Barney McCabe stopped, snorted and, with a big grin, headed slowly back towards his farm.

The back door of Ragtime's house opened. Mr and Mrs Pip, Thomas and Tillie gasped in amazement when right in front of them they saw a juggling blackbird, a cartwheeling frog, a whistling duck, a dancing mouse, a very talented snail named Angelo and . . . one very happy cat, Runaway Ragtime. He had returned home. And he wasn't planning to have any more adventures . . . well, not for a while anyway.

One, Two, Buckle My Shoe

One, two,
Buckle my shoe;
Three, four,
Knock at the door;
Five, six,
Pick up sticks;
Seven, eight;
Lay them straight;
Nine, ten,
A big fat hen;

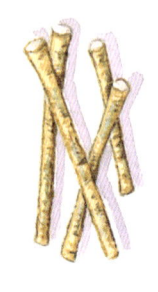

Eleven, twelve,
Dig and delve;
Thirteen, fourteen,
Maids a-courting;
Fifteen, sixteen,
Maids in the kitchen;
Seventeen, eighteen,
Maids in waiting;
Nineteen, twenty;
My plate's empty.

The Three Little Pigs and the Wolf

Early one morning
The sun came out,
And out set three pigs
Snorting their snouts.
SNORT!

Snort! *Snort!*

The three little pigs – Oink, Grunt and Curly – walked up the hills and down the dales until their cheeks were quite pink.

The Three Little Pigs and the Wolf

TEE-HEE!

They walked to the woods
Where the path split in three,
And the three little pigs said:
"TEE-HEE!"

TEE-HEE!

The pigs set off in different directions. Oink went this way, Grunt went that way and Curly went . . . well . . .

Curly felt sad
As she trotted alone,
But then found some straw
For building her home.
HOME!

When her house was finished, Curly gathered some extra straw to make a table and chair for the inside. And, last of all, she plaited a little straw bed so that she would have a cosy night's sleep. But . . .

Along came a wolf
With a scary big frown,
Sharp teeth and a huff
And a blow your house down.
DOWN!

Poor Curly. Her straw house was no more. How she ran and ran, up the hills and down the dales, to escape from that horrid wolf. Meanwhile,

Grunt snapped some sticks
From branches of wood
To make a new home
In the best way she could.
HOME!

When her house was finished, Grunt gathered some extra sticks to make a table and chair for the inside. And, last of all, she wove a little stick bed so that she would have a cosy night's sleep.
But . . .

Along came the wolf
With a scary big frown,
Sharp teeth and a huff
And a blow your house
DOWN!

Poor Grunt. Her stick house was no more. How she ran and ran, up the hills and down the dales, to escape from that horrid wolf.

Meanwhile,

Oink was struggling
With big heavy bricks,
But a brick house was stronger
Than a house made with sticks.
STICKS? POOH!

When her house was finished, Oink gathered some extra bricks to make a table and chair for the inside. And, last of all, she stacked some bricks for a little brick bed so that she would have a . . . well . . . probably extremely uncomfortable sleep that night.

Meanwhile . . . Curly and Grunt were still running, up hills and down dales, until their cheeks were quite pink. They were running to the place where their sister had built her house made of bricks.

Curly and Grunt ran,
Ran all the way,
Away from the wolf
To Oink's house to stay.
HOORAY! HOORAY!
HOORAY!
When, of course . . .

Along came the wolf
With a scary big frown,
Sharp teeth and a huff
And a blow your house down.
DOWN! NOT DOWN!

Inside the brick house, Oink, Grunt and Curly felt very safe.

Outside the brick house, the wolf's cheeks were growing redder and redder and hotter and hotter from all that huffing and puffing.

The brick house stayed up,
The wolf tumbled down,
Down a steep hill,
Still wearing his frown.
SNORT! SWEET! SNORT!

The Three Little Pigs and the Wolf ✦

When the wolf was gone, Grunt wove some sticks in a clever way to make three little chairs. Oink made two more brick beds – one for each of her sisters.

And Curly used her straw-plaiting skills to make a lovely soft mattress to put on top of the brick beds. And the three little pigs had a very cosy night's sleep.
Goodnight!

Polly Penguin Wants to Fly

Penguins are wonderful swimmers. They can dive down deep. They can twist and roll in the water. They can swim as fast as any fish. But no penguin has ever learned to fly.

"It's not fair!" says Polly Penguin, watching the gulls wheeling in the bright-blue sky above her head.

"I want to fly too. Like all the other birds."

"I want to fly," says Polly to her mother as they waddle out to join their friends on the big, steep ice slide.

"Don't be silly," says her mother. "This is much more fun!"

And then they both slide down on their tummies, all the way into the sea.

Wheeee!

"This is great fun," agrees Polly as they scramble out of the water. "But I still want to fly."

"Have you ever learned to fly?" Polly asks Wise Old Whale as he cruises along beside her.

"Not really," says Whale. "But every now and then I leap out of the water and fly through the air, just for a moment or two."

"I shall try that," says Polly, jumping out of the sea and sailing high into the air before landing on the ice again.

Wheeeeeee!

"That was great fun!" laughs Polly, as she runs to the edge of an iceberg with hundreds of other penguins and jumps into the sea.

Wheeeeeee!

"And so is this, but I still want to fly, too."

She lands with a big splash right next to Snowy, the white seal.

"Hello, Polly!" says Snowy.

"Hello, Snowy!" says Polly. "Have you ever learned to fly?"

"Not really," replies Snowy. "But every now and then I take a deep breath, stretch out my flippers, flick my tail and shoot through the water so fast that it feels as if I am flying, just for a moment or two."

"I shall try that," says Polly, flashing so fast through the waves that, just for a moment, she really does seem to be flying.

Wheeeeeee!

"Can you fly?" Polly asks Fluffy Rabbit as she scampers over the snow.

"Not really," says Fluffy Rabbit. "Although sometimes I jump so high that I think I might take off into the sky. But it is good to skip and hop just for fun sometimes. Will you join me?"

So Polly skips and jumps and hops and rolls in the snow with Fluffy until it is dark.

The air is turning icy cold and the stars are coming out as Polly sets off for home.

On the way she meets Reindeer, who is busy polishing his antlers in the snow.

"My mum says you are only here for a flying visit," says Polly. "So can you fly? Where are your wings?"

"No, little Polly, I am afraid that I cannot fly," answers Reindeer sadly. "Although there are stories about some lucky reindeers who can."

He stares up into the night sky.

"But now," he says, "it is getting very late. I think you should be at home, Polly. Your mum will be worried."

"Yes," says Polly, "I must hurry," and she scampers off, sliding over the ice.

"Wait!" calls Reindeer. "I can give you a ride." So Polly hops up onto Reindeer's back and she hangs on tightly to his antlers as he gallops all the way home.

"This is wonderful!" cries Polly.

The air rushes past her and they seem to fly through the night.

Wheeeeeee!

"Thank you," says Polly to Reindeer, sliding off his back by her front door. "That really did feel like flying. It was great. Can I have a ride again tomorrow?"

Reindeer nods. He is happy to have a new friend.

"Well, did you learn to fly today?" asks Dad, as Polly scuttles inside.

"Not exactly, not really. But . . . well, yes, in a way,"

replies Polly, smiling.

"Well, what a funny mixed-up answer!" laughs her father.

"Oh, I went so fast that it felt like flying," explains Polly. "And I was high up in the air – and it was just like magic."

"Good!" says Polly's mum. "Now it is time for supper. I have been flying around everywhere too – sliding and shopping and cooking. And your father has been jumping off icebergs and racing and fishing, so we have all had an exciting busy day. Now let's enjoy our fish supper together."

And they do.

As Polly eats her delicious fish, she dreams of riding on Reindeer's back again. One day, perhaps, if she is really lucky, she will meet those special reindeers who can really fly – and soar right up into the midnight sky. Wouldn't that be exciting?

Wee Willie Winkie

Wee Willie Winkie
Runs through the town,
Upstairs and downstairs
In his night-gown,
Rapping at the window,
Crying through the lock,
Are all the children in their beds,
For now it's eight o'clock?

I See the Moon

I see the moon,
And the moon sees me;
God bless the moon,
And God bless me.

Jack Be Nimble

Jack be nimble,
Jack be quick,
Jack jump over
The candlestick.

Go to Bed Late

Go to bed late,
Stay very small;
Go to bed early,
Grow very tall.